Cambridge Discovery Readers

Level 1

Series editor: Nichol

Amazing Young Sports People

Mandy Loader

CAMBRIDGE
UNIVERSITY PRESS

CAMBRIDGE
UNIVERSITY PRESS

79 Anson Road, #06-04/06, Singapore 079906

Cambridge University Press is part of the University of Cambridge.

It furthers the University's mission by disseminating knowledge in the pursuit of education, learning and research at the highest international levels of excellence.

www.cambridge.org
This American English edition is based on *Amazing Young Sports People*, ISBN 978-84-832-3572-0 first published by Cambridge University Press in 2009.

© Cambridge University Press 2009, 2010

First published 2009
American English edition 2010
Reprinted 2016

Printed in Italy by Rotolito Lombarda S.p.A.

ISBN 978-0-521-14899-3 Paperback American English edition

Mandy Loader would like to thank Hugh Sleight, Sebastián García and Tim Barnett for their kind help.

Illustrations by Aleix Pons Oliver

Edited by Carol Giscombe

Audio recording by hyphen

The publishers are grateful to the following for permission to reproduce photographic material:

Richard Price | Getty Images for cover image

Contents

Chapter 1

The Olympic Games

FACT

When: The first Olympic Games were in 776 BC.

Where: Olympia, Greece.

How often: Every four years.

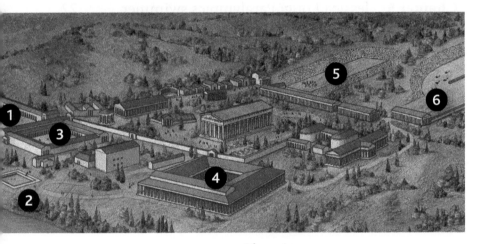

Olympia

1   Runners practiced here for the running races[1].
2   The swimming pool was only used for fun.
     There weren't any swimming races.
3   Athletes practiced here for the long jump competitions.
4   This hotel was for important people.
5   Forty thousand people sat in this stadium[2].
6   The horse races were here.

Thousands of people came to Olympia for the first Olympic Games. They came from lots of different towns in Greece.

At first there were only short running races. Later there were jumping competitions, boxing competitions, and also horse racing. The Games were fun. People sold food, drinks, and flowers. There were singers and dancers, too.

Only men played in the Games. In today's Olympics, athletes wear shorts and shirts, but in the first games, the athletes didn't wear anything. There weren't any women watching the Games!

In Greece, at that time, there was a lot of fighting[3]. But the Games started and everybody stopped fighting for a month. They went to the Games. Then the Games finished and people started fighting again.

There were Games at Olympia every four years for a thousand years. They stopped around 400 AD and didn't start again for almost 1,500 years.

Today there are two Olympic Games: the Summer Olympics and the Winter Olympics.

When: The modern Summer Olympic Games started in 1896. The Winter Olympics started in 1924.

Where: In different countries in the world.

How often: Every four years.

The modern Olympic Games aren't always in Greece. They're in a different country each time.

Thousands of athletes – men *and* women – come to the modern Olympics. They come from over two hundred different countries in the world. They all want to win medals for their countries: a gold medal is for first, a silver medal is for second, and a bronze medal is for third.

The Summer Olympics: Some of the competitions at the Summer Olympics are running, jumping, boxing, cycling, swimming, and horseback riding.

The Winter Olympics: Some of the competitions at the Winter Olympics are skiing, ski jumping, skating, ice hockey, and snowboarding.

In Olympia, a short time before the Olympic Games, eleven women light the flame on the Olympic torch. Then athletes take the torch from Olympia in Greece to the Olympic stadium. This can be a long run. Sometimes the Olympic torch needs to go on a ship[4] or a plane[5]. In 2008 over twenty thousand athletes took the torch from Olympia to Beijing, China.

After many days or weeks, the last athlete arrives and lights the big flame in the Olympic stadium. Now the Games can start!

the Olympic torch

Chapter 2

Amir Khan:
Olympic boxer

Name: Amir Khan
Sport: boxing
Job: boxer and student
Born: December 8, 1986
Height: 1.78 meters
Nationality: British
Lives: Bolton, near
Manchester, England
Likes: Muhammad Ali,
the American boxer –
Ali was World Champion
three times!

Boxers fight for short "rounds." A round is three minutes. After a round, the boxer can rest. At the Olympics there are usually three rounds. Some boxing matches can be twelve rounds. A boxer tries to knock the other boxer down[6]. A boxer can't be down for ten seconds, or the other boxer wins.

Amir Khan was always a fighter. He was in a lot of fights at school. When he was eight years old, his father took him to a boxing club. He enjoyed it and wanted to go again. His mother thought boxing was a dangerous sport and she wasn't happy. She liked soccer, but Amir didn't play very well. Amir went to the boxing club every week and he learned fast. Boxing helped him listen. He stopped fighting at school and he started listening to his teachers.

Amir started to fight in competitions when he was eleven. He went to school every day and he practiced every evening.

When Amir was seventeen, he went to the Summer Olympics in Athens, Greece. He was the only British boxer at the Olympics. He won a silver medal. He went back to England and a lot of people were at the airport. They wanted to take his picture and talk to him. Amir Kahn was famous.

Amir practices a lot. He watches other boxers and their fights. Then he copies them. After every fight, Amir sits down with his trainer and they talk about his mistakes[7]. Amir remembers them and he never makes the same mistake again.

Champions need to be in very good shape[8]. Amir can't eat chocolate or fast food and he needs to sleep a lot. He can't forget to study. He's studying physical education. He's rich now, but he still lives with his family.

People like Amir Khan – he has a lot of fans[9]. Many young people want to be a successful athlete like Amir.

"It's everyone's dream[10] to go to the Olympic Games."
—Amir Khan

How do you become a boxer?
Find a boxing club.
Practice every day.
Eat lots of fruit and vegetables.
Drink lots of water when you are practicing or boxing.
Sleep for eight hours every night.

- A head guard to protect your head.
- A mouth guard to protect your teeth.
- Boxing gloves to protect your hands.

Chapter 3

Sonja Henie:
Olympic figure skater

Name: Sonja Henie
Sport: figure skating
Job: figure skater and actress
Born: April 8, 1912
Died: October 12, 1969
Height: 1.60 meters
Nationality: Norwegian
Lived: Oslo, Norway and Los Angeles, U.S.A.

Sonja Henie started dancing lessons when she was five years old. She loved dancing and wanted to be a dancer. Then, on her sixth birthday, she got some ice skates and she started skating. Now she wanted to dance *and* skate.

Sonja decided to be a figure skater.

Her brother Leif gave her lessons at first. She learned very fast and she was very good. Then her parents spoke to a famous skating teacher, Oscar Holte. He began to give her lessons and Sonja won the children's figure skating championship in Oslo when she was eight years old. At ten she won the national figure skating championship of Norway.

At eleven Sonja went to her first Winter Olympic Games. She didn't skate very well. She forgot some of her turns and jumps. She finished eighth in the skating competition and she didn't win a medal. But she didn't give up[11].

fourteen-year-old Sonja Henie (1927)

Then Sonja saw Anna Pavlova, the famous Russian dancer. Sonja thought that Anna's dancing was beautiful. She wanted to copy[12] Anna Pavlova – on ice. She practiced for hours every day.

Two years later she went to the world championships in Stockholm. This time, she didn't forget her jumps and turns. She finished second. After the competition she said, "I didn't win this time, but next year I will and I'll never lose again."

And she didn't.

When she was sixteen, Sonja went to the Winter Olympics again. This time she won a gold medal. Her skating was new, beautiful, and interesting. The other skaters wore long skirts and brown boots, but Sonja wore a short skirt and white boots. She was different and everybody loved her skating. Sonja won a gold medal at the next two Winter Olympics. In her life, she won three Olympic Gold medals and ten world championships!

Sonja Henie changed the sport of figure skating. Thanks to her, thousands of young people started to buy skates and dance on ice.

A sportsperson ... and an actress

Sonja loved skating, but she loved tennis, too. She won three tennis championships.

She could also swim and ride horses very well, and she sometimes drove sports cars in races!

After her third Olympic gold medal, Sonja stopped skating in competitions. She went to Hollywood and became an actress. She made a lot of movies – often about skaters. She died very rich and very famous.

How do you start figure skating?

Find an ice rink.

Find a trainer.

Take figure skating classes.

What does a figure skater need?

costume

figure skates

- Figure skates (different from other skates – they help you jump and turn).
- Figure skaters often wear costumes when they are skating.

ACTIVITIES

● ●

1 Complete the sentences about Chapter 1 with the numbers in the box.

11	20,000	40,000	200
400	~~776~~	1896	1924

1 The Olympic Games started in ....776...... BC, in Greece.
2 At the first Olympic Games, there were .... seats in the stadium.
3 The Olympic Games stopped around .... AD.
4 The modern Olympic Games started in ....
5 The Winter Olympics started in ....
6 Athletes from over .... countries come to the modern Olympic Games.
7 .... women in Olympia light the flame on the Olympic torch.
8 More than .... athletes carried the Olympic torch from Olympia to Beijing.

2 Are the sentences about Chapter 1 true (*T*) or false (*F*)?

1 There were swimming competitions in the first Olympic Games. ☒F☐
2 There were boxing competitions at the Olympic Games in 776. ☐
3 In the first Olympics there were no women athletes. ☐
4 The first Olympic Games started and fighting stopped in Greece for a month. ☐
5 Snowboarding isn't an Olympic sport. ☐
6 The Olympic torch sometimes travels by ship. ☐

16

3 Match the sentences to the people in the box.

> Amir (x4)   Sonja (x3)

1 ....Sonja.... didn't do well at her / his first Olympics.
2 .... started competitions at the age of eleven.
3 .... started the sport at the age of eight.
4 The sport helped .... at school.
5 .... won a gold medal at her / his second Olympics.
6 .... won a silver medal at her / his first Olympics.
7 .... wore different clothes than other people to do the sport.

4 Answer the questions.

1 What does Amir Khan do after fights?

....

2 What is Amir studying?

....

3 Sonja Henie loved skating. What else did she love doing?

....

4 What did Sonja do after she stopped skating?

....

LOOKING FORWARD

• •

5 Check (✓) what you think is true about the Paralympics.

1 The Paralympics are every three years. ☐
2 The Paralympic Games do not use the same stadium as the Olympics. ☐

Chapter 4

The Paralympic Games

FACT

When: The first Summer Paralympic Games were in 1960; the first Winter Paralympics were in 1976.

Where: In the same countries as the Summer and Winter Olympic Games.

How often: Every four years, after the Olympic Games.

One sport at the Paralympics is wheelchair basketball.

The Paralympic Games are for physically disabled[13] athletes. Paralympic athletes have many different disabilities. Some Paralympic athletes can't walk or run. They play their sport in wheelchairs.

At the Paralympics there are lots of wheelchair sports – for example, wheelchair tennis, wheelchair basketball, and wheelchair rugby. The athletes have special wheelchairs. They can go very fast. There are also wheelchair races at the Paralympics. Sometimes athletes go at thirty kilometers an hour.

In 2008 disabled athletes carried the Olympic flame from Olympia to Beijing and, at the start of the Paralympics, a disabled high jump champion, Hou Bin, lit the Olympic flame. Hou Bin was in a wheelchair. He couldn't run up and light the flame. Slowly, he pulled his wheelchair seventy meters into the air and lit the flame. It was very difficult, but he did it – and then the Paralympic Games started!

The Paralympic Games start two weeks after the Olympic Games, in the same city. The Paralympics use the same stadium as the Olympics. Lots of the sports are the same in the Paralympics and the Olympics.

Some Paralympic records are almost the same as Olympic records. For example, the Olympic record for the men's 100-meter running race is 9.69 seconds and the record for the women's 100-meters is 10.49 seconds. The Paralympic 100-meter men's record is 10.96 seconds.

Blind athletes run with help from seeing athletes.

In the first Paralympic Games, there were only four hundred athletes from twenty-three countries. They played twelve different sports. Now the Games are very big. In 2008 there were over 4,000 athletes from 145 countries and there were twenty different sports.

the Beijing Paralympics in 2008

Chapter 5

Jessica Long:
Paralympic swimmer

Name: Jessica Tatiana Long
Sport: swimming
Job: student
Born: February 29, 1992
Nationality: American
Lives: Baltimore, U.S.A.
Favorite food: pizza
Likes: going to the
movies, shopping,
bike riding, cooking

Jessica Long is a very fast Paralympic swimmer. She was born in Russia with a disability. This was difficult for her mother and Jessica lived in a special house for children.

When Jessica was thirteen months old, an American couple, Steve and Beth Long, visited this house. They wanted a child and they thought Jessica was beautiful. They adopted her and took her to the U.S.A. with them. Jessica had a new mom and dad.

When Jessica was eighteen months old, doctors said she had to lose her legs below the knee. The doctors gave Jessica artificial[14] legs and she learned to walk for the first time. Jessica and her parents were very happy.

When she was a young child, Jessica loved sports. She learned to swim in her grandparents' swimming pool. At the age of ten, she started to swim in competitions. "She was always the first person in the swimming pool and the last person out of it," says her father.

At twelve, Jessica went to her first Paralympic Games in Greece. Her family went with her because she was very young.

Nobody thought Jessica could win, but they were wrong. She won three gold medals!

At fourteen, Jessica went to the World Swimming Championships in Durban, South Africa. She won nine more gold medals and she broke five world records!

At sixteen, at the Beijing Paralympic Games, she won four gold medals, two silver medals, and a bronze medal. She also broke three more world records!

Swimmers from over eighty countries swim in the Paralympic Games.

Jessica likes other sports, too. She enjoys running and, at fourteen, she started rock climbing[15]. Four months later she went to an international competition in the U.S.A. She finished second!

Jessica Long is an amazing young athlete. How does she do it?

"I love winning and I'm not going to give up."

—*Jessica Long*

Chapter 6

Ricardo Alves:
Paralympic soccer player

Name: Ricardo Alves
Sport: blind soccer
Job: student
Born: December 15, 1988
Nationality: Brazilian
Likes: Kaká (a Brazilian soccer player)

blind soccer at the 2008
Beijing Paralympics

Blind soccer is a fast and exciting[16] game.

There are five players on a team.

Each half of the game is twenty-five minutes long.

The soccer ball has a bell in it – blind soccer players can't see the ball, but they can hear it!

They don't play on a grass soccer field; they play on a hard field because they need to hear the ball on the ground.

The goalkeepers have to stay near the goal. They *can* see – they are not blind. The coaches can see too, and they shout and help the players.

The fans cannot shout, or the players won't hear the coach or the ball!

FACT

The soccer field isn't very big. The players can't lose the ball because there is a wall around it.

Ricardo Alves started playing soccer at the age of two. He often played with his brother. He loved soccer and he wanted to play all the time. But, at the age of eight, he went blind. Ricardo was very sad, but he didn't want to give up soccer. He learned to play blind soccer. Now he plays blind soccer for Brazil.

Ricardo first played for Brazil when he was sixteen. The competition was the American Cup for the Blind. In the first game, Brazil played Paraguay. Brazil won 3–0 and Ricardo scored all three goals – a hat trick[17]! Then he scored six goals against Bolivia! In the same year, Ricardo played for Brazil in the World Cup for the Blind. Brazil lost the final[18], but Ricardo played very well.

When he was nineteen, Brazil played in the Pan American Games. Brazil played Argentina. This time Brazil won and Ricardo was the top scorer in the competition. He scored nine goals.

Ricardo Alves in the Pan American Games

At twenty, Ricardo played in the Paralympic Games in Beijing. There were six teams competing for the gold medal and Brazil played China in the final. There were two thousand people at the game. The people watching couldn't shout – they stayed very quiet, but it wasn't easy!

China scored the first goal, but then Ricardo scored a goal for Brazil. Then, just twenty-five seconds before the game finished, Brazil scored a second goal. They were Paralympic Champions for the second time!

Ricardo said it was a difficult game. The Chinese team was very good and they were playing at home.

After the Paralympics, Ricardo went home. Lots of students and teachers from his school were at his house – they wanted to take him to school on a fire engine!

Ricardo loves music and plays the guitar and other musical instruments. He's also a very good student at school and wants to study physical education in college. And, of course, he still wants to play soccer for Brazil!

LOOKING BACK

• •

1 Check your answers to *Looking forward* on page 17.

ACTIVITIES

• •

2 Match the two parts of the sentences about Chapter 4.

1 In wheelchair races, athletes sometimes go at [e]
2 The Paralympics start ☐
3 The Paralympics record for the men's 100-meter running race is ☐
4 In the first Paralympics, there were ☐
5 In the 2008 Paralympics, there were athletes from ☐

a two weeks after the Olympics.
b 145 countries.
c 10.96 seconds.
d four hundred athletes.
e thirty kilometers an hour.

3 Underline the correct answer to complete the information from Chapter 5.

1 Jessica Long is a ... .
a swimmer   b cyclist   c runner

2 Steve and Beth Long took Jessica to ... .
a Russia   b America   c Greece

3 Jessica started to swim in competitions at the age of ... .
a ten   b fourteen   c twelve

4 At the Beijing Paralympics, Jessica won ... gold medals.
a nine   b four   c three

4 Complete the sentences with information from Chapter 6.

1 There are ....*five*........ players on a team.

2 A game is .... minutes long.

3 There's a .... in the ball.

4 They play on a .... field, not grass.

5 Goalkeepers are not ....

6 Fans cannot ....

7 There's a .... around the field.

5 Write Ricardo Alves' age, using information from Chapter 7.

1 At the age of ....*two*........, Ricardo Alves started playing soccer.

2 He became blind when he was ....

3 At .... , he first played for Brazil.

4 He scored nine goals in the Pan American Games when he was ....

5 At .... , he played in the Paralympic Games in Beijing.

LOOKING FORWARD

• •

6 What do you think? Answer the questions.

1 Where are the X Games?

2 How often are the Games?

3 What sports are in the X Games?

Chapter 7

The X Games

FACT

When: The first Summer X Games were in 1995. The first Winter X Games were in 1997.

Where: The Summer and Winter X Games are in the U.S.A.

How often: Every year, usually in January and August.

Extreme sports are difficult and they can also be very dangerous.

The X Games are for extreme action sports. Extreme sports are very different from Olympic sports. In the X Games, athletes do special tricks.

In the Summer X Games, athletes do tricks on motorcycles, bikes, skates, and skateboards.

In the Winter X Games, athletes do tricks on skis and snowboards and have races on snowbikes.

Snowboarding is one of the sports at the Winter X Games.

Extreme sports can be dangerous. Athletes often break their arms or legs. But sometimes they're lucky. Jake Brown is an Australian skateboarder. At one X Games he tried a very difficult trick. He was the first person to do this trick at the X Games. But then he fell – fifteen meters! After a short time, he got up and waved to his fans. He was OK. Jake was very lucky.

People love watching the X Games. Every year there is something new to see – new tricks and sometimes new sports. They are always extreme and they are always special.

At the Winter X Games, there is a skate park. Everybody – the athletes and the fans – can go to the park and have fun. There is also a big party or festival every year, the X Fest, with lots of music concerts.

The X Games are very popular in America. In the first year of the Winter X Games, 38,000 people watched them. Two years later, 83,000 people went to watch the Games!

Travis Pastrana does amazing tricks on a motorcycle.

Some athletes at the X Games enjoy the danger.

Travis Pastrana is a motorcycle champion. When Travis was only fifteen, he got ninety-nine out of a hundred for his first trick. Then, he did another amazing trick.

He started to ride his motorcycle slowly. There was a very tall ramp in front of him. He began to go faster. He went up the ramp very fast – but he didn't stop at the top. He went off the top of the ramp and he flew through the air – on his bike. Then he fell twenty-five meters into the ocean. It was a very exciting trick.

Chapter 8

Ayumi Kawasaki: extreme in-line skater

Name: Ayumi Kawasaki
Sport: in-line skating
Job: student and professional[19] skater
Born: July 27, 1984
Height: 1.52 meters
Nationality: Japanese
Lives: Higashi, Japan
Favorite city: Los Angeles, California, U.S.A.
Favorite food: fish
Likes: hip hop and learning English

In the X Games the in-line skaters skate on a wall. The wall is like a big "U." The competitors skate up the wall and fly off the top. Then they do tricks in the air. They have to go up very high in the air and their tricks have to be very difficult. Then they have to skate on the wall again and they can't fall. They have to do all their tricks in one minute.

When Ayumi Kawasaki was nine, she saw a movie about in-line skating. She loved it and wanted to skate, too. After three years she was a very good skater. She could do lots of jumps and tricks because she was small and light.

She started skating in competitions in different countries. She became a professional at twelve and she won a lot of money. She did some difficult and dangerous tricks, but she was very lucky and she didn't have any bad falls.

She first skated in the X Games in San Diego, California when she was twelve and she won a bronze medal. The next year she tried again, and won a silver medal. The year after that, she went to the X Games in San Francisco U.S.A., and won a gold medal. She was only fourteen years old!

How did Ayumi become a champion? It wasn't easy. She went to the skate park after school every day and she practiced for three or four hours. After this she went back to her house, tired and hungry. She had dinner, did her homework, and went to bed.

extreme skating at the X Games

Ayumi didn't talk about being famous. Her friends at school knew Ayumi liked skating, but they didn't know she was a champion!

Ayumi Kawasaki on a U-pipe

What do you need to be an in-line skater?

helmet

elbow pads

wrist guards

knee pads

in-line skates

- A helmet to protect your head.
- Wrist guards, knee pads, and elbow pads to protect your wrists, knees, and elbows.
- In-line skates with four wheels in a line.

Chapter 9

Ryan Sheckler: extreme street skateboarder

Name: Ryan Sheckler
Sport: skateboarding
Job: professional skater
Born: December 30, 1989
Height: 1.73 meters
Nationality: American
Lives: San Clemente, California, U.S.A.
Favorite food: chicken
Likes: rap music, heavy metal, movies, surfing, snowboarding, golf, and riding motorcycles
Hates: doing the dishes!

Ryan Sheckler found his father's old skateboard when he was eighteen months old. He took the skateboard everywhere with him. One day, when he was four years old, he stood on the board and started skateboarding.

He wanted to learn to do tricks. At the age of six, he was on the skateboard for twenty-two hours a week. When Ryan did his first trick, his father was very happy and he made a small skate park for Ryan. Ryan and his friends skated in the skate park for many years.

At eight, he was already a very good street skater. He skated fast. He knew lots of tricks and he was never afraid of falling. He started skateboarding in competitions and he won a lot of championships.

Ryan Sheckler at the 2008 X Games in Los Angeles

He stopped going to school at twelve because he didn't have time to go to school and to skate. Teachers went to his house and taught him in the morning. Science and math were his favorite subjects. Then, in the afternoon, he practiced skateboarding.

Ryan became a professional skater when he was very young – just thirteen! He went to the X Games in Los Angeles, California, and won a gold medal. In the next few years, he won a lot of skateboarding competitions. He was only sixteen years old when he became "Athlete of the Year." Then, at nineteen, he won gold at the X Games again!

FACT

In the X Games, street skaters jump over ramps and boxes on the street.

At the age of eighteen, Ryan had his own TV show. Its name was *Life of Ryan*. The show was about Ryan, his skateboarding, and his family. Over 41 million people watched the show. Ryan has a lot of fans! What's his advice?

"Just go out there and have fun."
—*Ryan Sheckler*

- A skateboard (it isn't easy to stand on!).
- Skate shoes (special shoes for skateboarding).
- Ramps to help you do tricks.
- Wrist guards, knee pads, and elbow pads to protect your wrists, knees, and elbows.

LOOKING BACK

• •

1 Check your answers to *Looking forward* on page 31.

ACTIVITIES

• •

2 Complete the sentences about Chapter 7 with the words in the box.

> motorcycle ~~action sports~~ new sports
> skateboarder tricks

1 The X Games are games for extreme _action sports_ .

2 In the X Games, athletes do special ....

3 Jake Brown is an Australian ....

4 The X Games change – they often have ....

5 Travis Pastrana is a .... champion.

3 Answer the questions.

1 What sports do athletes do in the Summer X Games?

....

2 What can often happen to athletes in the X Games?

....

3 How far did Jake Brown fall?

....

4 What happens at the X Fest?

....

5 How far did Travis Pastrana fall?

....

4 <u>Underline</u> the correct words in each sentence about in-line skating.

1 In competitions, skaters do tricks *on the wall / in the air.*

2 Competitors *have to / don't have to* go very high in the air.

3 In competitions, you have *one minute / two minutes* to do the tricks.

4 In-line skates have *two / four* wheels in a line.

5 Skaters *wear / don't wear* a helmet.

5 Match the facts to the people in the box.

| Ayumi (x4)   Ryan (x3) |

1 ....*Ryan*.... became professional at the age of thirteen.

2 ....'s favorite food is fish.

3 .... won a bronze medal at her / his first X Games.

4 .... friends did not know she / he was a champion.

5 .... started the sport at the age of four.

6 .... stopped going to school at the age of twelve.

7 .... won a gold medal at the age of fourteen.

6 <u>Underline</u> the correct answer to complete the information from Chapter 9.

1 Ryan was born in December, ...
   a <u>1989</u>   b 1984   c 1988

2 He lives in ... .
   a San Clemente   b Los Angeles   c Baltimore

3 More than ... million people watched Ryan's TV show.
   a 16   b 41   c 22

4 Ryan's advice is to "Just go out there and ... ."
   a practice a lot   b win medals   c have fun

Glossary

[1]**race** (page 4) *noun*   a running competition

[2]**stadium** (page 4) *noun*   a big area with seats around it – people play or watch sports here

[3]**fighting** (page 5) *noun*   when people try to hurt or kill each other

[4]**ship** (page 7) *noun*   a big boat

[5]**plane** (page 7) *noun*   a machine that flies; an airplane

[6]**knock down** (page 8) *phrasal verb*   to hit someone very hard, so that the person falls to the ground

[7]**mistake** (page 10) *noun*   something that you do or think which is wrong

[8]**to be in good shape** (page 10) *adjective*   healthy, especially because you eat well and do sports

[9]**fan** (page 10) *noun*   someone who likes a famous person, sport, type of music, etc.

[10]**dream** (page 10) *noun*   (here) something you want to happen very much

[11]**give up** (page 13) *phrasal verb*   to stop doing something because it is very difficult

[12]**copy** (page 14) *verb*   to do the same things as another person

[13]**disabled** (page 19) *adjective*   having a condition or problem which makes it difficult to do the things that other people do

[14]**artificial** (page 23) *adjective*   not natural or real

[15]**rock climbing** (page 25) *noun*   a sport in which people climb up or across real or artificial mountains or walls

[16]**exciting** (page 26) *adjective*   making you feel very happy and interested

[17]**hat trick** (page 27) *noun*   when somebody scores three goals or points in soccer and other sports

[18]**final** (page 27) *noun*   the last game in a competition to decide the winner

[19]**professional** (page 36) *adjective*   someone is professional if they get money for the sport they play

The authors and publishers are grateful to the following for permission to use copyright material. All efforts have been made to contact the copyright holders of material reproduced in this book which belongs to third parties, and citations are given for the sources. We welcome approaches from any copyright holders whom we have not been able to trace but who find that their material has been reproduced herein.

p6©MICHAEL REYNOLDS/epa/Corbis; p7 ©Titania 1980|dreamstime.com; p8 ©Getty/SHAUN CURRY; p9 ©PA Wire/PA Photos/Cordon Press; p12 ©Keystone/ Getty Images; p13 ©2002 Topham Picturepoint/Cordon Press; p18 ©Xinhua/Imago/ Icon SMI; p19 ©Getty/Jamie McDonald; p20 ©Xinhua/Photoshot/Cordon Press; p21 ©imago/Xinhua/Cordon Press; p22 (close-up) ©Getty/Matthew Stockman; p22 (swimming) ©Xinhua/Landov/Cordon Press; p23 ©REUTERS/Cordon Press; p24 ©Getty/China Photos; p26 (close-up) ©Sol Neelman/Corbis; p26 (soccer) ©Yan Sheng – CNImaging/Cordon Press; p28 ©REUTERS/Bruno Domingos/Cordon Press; p32 ©Getty/Jonathan Moore; p33 ©Stanley Hu/Icon SMI; p34 ©Marc Piscotty/ Icon SMI; p35 ©REUTERS/Phil McCarten/Cordon Press; p36 ©photo courtesy of Good Skates, Inc.; p37 ©Zach Podell/Icon SMI; p38 ©Getty/Tom Hauck; p40 ©AXELLE/BAUER-GRIFFIN.COM/Cordon Press; p41 ©Tony Donaldson/Icon SMI